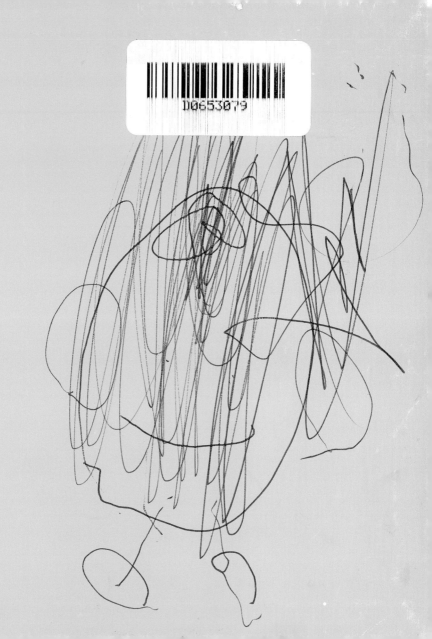

D0653079

The Usborne Little Book of Fairy Things to Make and Do

Rebecca Gilpin and
Catherine Atkinson

Designed by Katrina Fearn and Nicola Butler
Illustrated by Jan McCafferty, Lucy Parris and Molly Sage
Photographs by Howard Allman
Cover design by Erica Harrison

Contents

Fairy cooking

Funky fairies

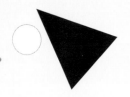

1. Cut a round head from thin white cardboard. Then, cut a triangle from bright cardboard, for the fairy's body.

2. Cut two bright paper triangles for hair. Then, cut curves along the bottom edges and round off the points at the top.

3. Glue the head onto the body, and glue the hair onto the head, so that the pieces touch at the top. Then, draw a face.

4. Cut a square of pink net for the fairy's wings. Then, cut a long piece of thin, bright ribbon to hang the fairy from.

5. Scrunch the middle of the netting and tie it with one end of the ribbon. Then, cut two long pieces of ribbon, for legs.

6. Turn the body over, and tape the wings onto it, with the long piece of ribbon pointing up. Then, tape the legs on, too.

You could make lots of different fairies.

7. To make the arms, bend the bumpy part of a drinking straw and cut it so that both ends are the same length, like this.

8. Press the bumpy part of the straw onto a piece of poster tack. Then, press it onto the back of the fairy, just above the wings.

9. For feet, thread beads onto the fairy's legs and tie knots below them. Then, press a sticker onto her hair and hang her up.

Fairyland painting

Toadstools

1. Lay some paper towels onto some newspaper. Spread red or pink paint on the paper towels with the back of an old spoon.

2. Cut a potato in half, then carefully cut away the two sides, like this, to make a handle. Press the potato into the paint.

3. Press the potato onto a piece of paper. Then, dip a finger in white paint and print some spots. Using a brush, paint a white stalk.

Daisies and dandelions

1. Cut two small pieces of thick cardboard. To print daisies, dip the edge of one piece in white paint and press it on the paper.

2. Print lots more lines and cross them over each other, to make petals. Then, paint a yellow dot in the middle of each daisy.

3. Dip the long edge of the other piece of cardboard in yellow paint and print dandelions. Then, paint stalks and leaves.

Dragonflies

1. To paint a body, dip a fingertip into some paint and drag your finger quickly across the paper. Then, fingerpaint a head.

2. Clean your finger, then dip it in some white paint and drag it to make four wings. Then, add eyes with a felt-tip pen.

...dd some fingerpainted ...ries to your picture. ...nt their arms and legs ...th a piece of cardboard.

Print some toadstools first, then add flowers in the spaces.

Fairy wands

Sparkly star wand

1. Draw a star on a piece of cardboard. Cut it out, then lay it on another piece of cardboard and draw around it twice.

2. Cut out the stars and paint them on one side. Then, cut 10 pieces of thin ribbon which are half as long as a drinking straw.

3. Lay one of the stars on some scrap paper. Then, cover the side which has not been painted with household glue (PVA).

The paper protects the book.

4. Carefully lay the straw and pieces of ribbon on top of the glue, like this. Then, gently glue the other star on top.

5. Lay a sheet of paper over the star. Then, put a heavy book on top, and leave the wand for an hour, for the glue to dry.

6. Glue lots of sequins, glitter and tiny beads onto one side of the wand. Wait for it to dry, then decorate the other side.

8

Silver star wand

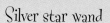
Make patterns with the string.

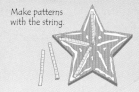

1. Cut out two stars and cover one side of each one with household glue (PVA). Then, press pieces of string onto the glue.

2. Lay a piece of kitchen foil over each star and gently rub all over it. The pattern of the pieces of string appears.

3. When the glue is dry, cut around the stars, leaving a border. Then, cut off the foil at the points, like this.

4. Cut little triangles into the border, like this. Then, bend the border up onto the star, until the edges of the star are covered.

5. Glue pieces of ribbon and a straw onto the back of one star. Then, glue the other star on the top and leave it to dry.

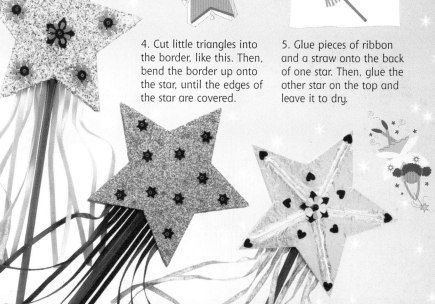

Snowflake fairies

1. Lay a mug on a piece of white paper. Draw around it, then draw around it on some purple paper, too. Then, cut out the circles.

2. To make a snowflake for the dress, fold the white circle in half, then fold it in half twice more. Then, cut a triangle out of one side.

3. Cut out lots more triangles, all around the edges of the folded piece of paper. Make the triangles different sizes.

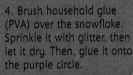

4. Brush household glue (PVA) over the snowflake. Sprinkle it with glitter, then let it dry. Then, glue it onto the purple circle.

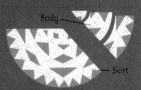

Body

Skirt

5. Cut the snowflake in half. For a skirt, cut one half into two pieces. Then, cut a shape for the body from the smaller piece.

6. Glue the skirt onto a piece of paper, then glue on the body. Cut out a purple sash and glue it on where the pieces join.

The fold needs to be on this side.

7. For the wings, draw around the mug and cut out the circle. Fold it in half three times, then draw half a wing shape, like this.

You could make a Christmas card with a snowflake fairy on it.

Keep the paper folded.

Add glittery shoes, too.

8. Cut along the line you have drawn, then cut a few triangles along the fold, like this. Then, open out the wings.

9. Spread glue over the wings. Sprinkle them with glitter, then let the glue dry. Glue the wings next to the body, like this.

10. Cut out a head and some hair and glue them together. Cut out arms, legs and a crown and glue them all on. Then, draw a face.

Printed fairies

To make a butterfly, cut wings from paper and fold them.

1. Glue a sponge cloth onto a piece of thin cardboard. This helps to make it less messy when you print.

2. Draw a triangle for the body on the cardboard. Then, put a small bottle top on the cardboard and draw around it.

3. Cut around the shapes, through the cardboard and the sponge. Then, lay some paper towels onto some newspaper.

4. Spread white paint on the paper towels, using the back of an old spoon. Then, lay the sponge side of the triangle in the paint.

12

5. Press the sponge onto a sheet of paper, rub the back gently, then lift it off. Print a head, then print more fairies.

6. From thin paper, cut enough wing shapes for each fairy to have two. Then, fold each wing in half and open it out.

7. Mix yellow and white paint together to make pale yellow. Then, press the edge of a piece of thick cardboard into the paint.

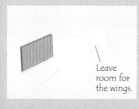

Leave room for the wings.

The wings stand out a little.

8. Press the cardboard onto the paper to print hair. Then, use another piece of cardboard to print arms and legs.

9. Paint the fairies' hands and feet and add their faces. Then, spread glue on one half of each wing, and press them on.

To give a fairy curved legs or arms, bend the cardboard before you print.

13

Flowery fairy wall-hanging

1. Lay a plate on a piece of thick white cardboard. Then, draw around the plate with a pencil and cut out the circle.

2. Using the pencil, lightly draw a line across the circle. Then, draw the outline of a rainbow and a sun at the top.

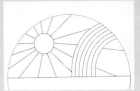

3. Add stripes to the rainbow and lots of lines for the sun's rays, like this. Then, paint bright stripes on the rainbow.

4. Paint the sun and its rays with two shades of yellow paint. Then, paint the ground and leave the paint to dry.

5. Draw lots of flowers on white paper, cut them out and paint yellow circles on them. Then, glue some of them onto the ground.

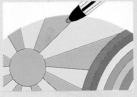

6. Using the point of a ballpoint pen, carefully make a small hole near the top of the painted circle, like this.

Don't glue flowers at the top of the ribbons.

7. Cut nine long pieces of thin bright ribbon and glue lots of paper flowers onto them. Then, leave the glue to dry.

8. Tape the pieces of ribbon around the bottom of the circle, making sure that you leave gaps between them.

9. Thread a piece of ribbon through the hole in the top of the circle, and tie it in a knot. Then, hang up your wall-hanging.

If you don't want to make a hole in your picture, tape a piece of ribbon to the back instead.

You could draw around the outlines with a silver pen or glitter glue.

You can also hang funky fairies on your wall-hanging (see pages 4-5).

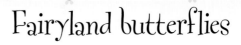

Fairyland butterflies

Salt-speckled butterflies

1. Paint all over a sheet of thick white paper with watery paint. Then, sprinkle grains of salt onto the paint and let it dry.

2. When the paint is dry, brush off the salt. Fold the paper in half and glue it together with the paint on the outside.

The fold needs to be on this side.

3. Fold the paper in half again. Draw two butterfly wings on it, then cut around the wings, through all the layers of paper.

4. For each butterfly, cut the end off a drinking straw, just above the bumpy part. To make feelers, cut down into the bumpy part.

Snip here.

5. Bend the feelers outward, then open the wings. Lay the straw in the fold, then snip off the bottom end of the straw.

Make sure the bead is wider than the straw.

6. Push a piece of ribbon through a bead. Tie a knot in the ribbon and push it through the straw. Glue the straw onto the wings.

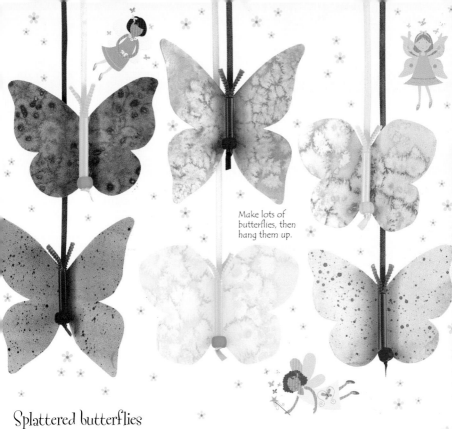

Make lots of
butterflies, then
hang them up.

Splattered butterflies

1. Paint all over a sheet
of thick white paper with
watery paint and let it dry.
Then, put some bright
paint on an old plate.

2. Dip a dry paintbrush
into the paint, then hold
it over the paper. Pull a
finger over the bristles, to
splatter the paint.

3. Splatter paint all over
the paper and let it dry.
Then, make two butterflies
by following the steps on
the opposite page.

Fairy door sign

Keep this quarter for later.

Remove these parts.

1. Put a small plate onto a sheet of paper and draw around it with a pencil. Then, cut out the circle you have drawn.

2. Fold the circle in half, then in half again, and open it out. Then, cut along two of the folds and remove one quarter.

3. Draw two wings touching the folds. Then, cut around the wings and along the folds to make the wings, like this.

The body stands out from the paper.

4. Decorate the body and the wings. Push the wings together, so that the body curves, then glue them onto some thick paper.

Kate's Room

5. Cut out a head and draw a face. Then, cut out hair and glue it on. Draw two arms on the paper quarter you kept earlier.

Asha's Room

You could glue your fairy onto a heart. Leave room to write your name.

Decorate the sign with shiny stickers.

Decorate the arms.

6. Cut out the arms. Then, cut hands and glue them onto the arms. Glue the arms and the head onto the body.

7. For legs, cut two long strips of paper. Make one end of each leg rounded, then fold the legs lots of times, to make zigzags.

8. Glue the legs under the body, with the rounded ends at the bottom. Then, write your name above the fairy.

Sparkly fairy wings

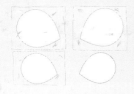

1. Draw two big wing shapes and two smaller ones on paper. Then, cut them out and lay plastic foodwrap over them.

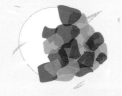

2. Rip up two shades of tissue paper and overlap the pieces on the plastic. Cover the wing shapes, including their edges.

3. Mix some household glue (PVA) with water so that it is runny. Then, paint glue all over the pieces of tissue paper.

4. Press on another layer of tissue paper and paint it with glue. Then, add about five more layers of tissue paper and glue.

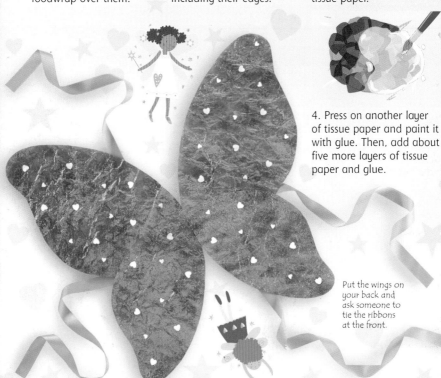

Put the wings on your back and ask someone to tie the ribbons at the front.

Press on shiny stickers to make the wings even more sparkly.

5. Sprinkle the top layer of glue with glitter. When it is dry, paint another layer of glue over the glitter. Leave the glue to dry.

6. Peel the tissue wings off the foodwrap. Lay the paper wings on top, then draw around them and cut out the shapes.

Leave long ends on the ribbons.

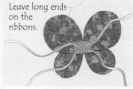

7. Glue the wings together, like this. Then, while the glue is drying, cut a small rectangle from a piece of thick cardboard.

8. Using a ballpoint pen, carefully make four holes in the rectangle. Then, thread two long pieces of ribbon through the holes.

9. Glue the rectangle onto the back of the wings, with the ends of the ribbons sticking out. Then, leave the glue to dry.

Flying fairies scene

To make a picture like this, paint toadstools and a fairy castle, then add fairies and flowers.

1. Mix a little orange and pink paint with water, and paint a face. Then, paint a bright pink shape below it for the body, like this.

2. Paint two paler shapes at the top of the fairy's body, for the wings. Then, paint a yellow shape for the hair and a circle for the wand.

3. Leave the paint to dry completely. Then, use a black felt-tip pen to add outlines to the fairy's head, body and wings.

More ideas

4. Draw a face, then add arms, legs and lines on the fairy's hair. Then, draw a wand with a star on the end, like this.

Piled-up

Spiky

Wavy

Try painting different hairstyles. Paint a tall shape for piled-up hair, zigzags for spiky hair and curly lines for wavy hair.

Round nose

Freckly

Surprised

Try different faces, too. A few dots make freckles, a round mouth looks surprised and noses could be round or pointed.

Fairy puppets

This side of the wing needs to be on the fold.

1. Fold a piece of thick paper in half. Draw a wing shape on it, like this. Then, keeping the paper folded, cut out the shape.

2. Open the wings and flatten them. Then, cut a shape for the fairy's body and arms from some bright paper.

3. Cut a paper circle for the head and a shape for the hair. Then, glue the hair onto the head and draw a face.

To make your puppets look different, try giving them different dresses and hair.

4. Cut out hands from paper and glue them onto the back of the fairy's arms. Then, glue the head onto the body.

Use pens and stickers to decorate the fairy.

5. Glue the body onto the wings, then decorate the fairy. Turn the fairy over and tape a straw onto the back of the body.

Fairy queen

Make a wand from thick paper and decorate the fairy queen with lots of stickers.

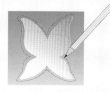

1. Cut a pair of wings from thick paper and lay them on another piece of paper. Draw bigger wings around them, like this.

2. Cut out the wings and glue the smaller wings onto them. Then, cut a long dress, a head, hair and hands from paper.

Draw a face.

3. Glue all the pieces onto the wings. Then, cut a crown from shiny paper and glue it on. Tape a straw onto the back.

Fairy palace

Add extra
decorations to
the palace with
a gold pen.

You could add
some printed fairies
from pages 12-13.

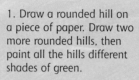

1. Draw a rounded hill on a piece of paper. Draw two more rounded hills, then paint all the hills different shades of green.

2. For the palace, cut a square and two towers from some paper. Make them small enough to fit on one of the hills.

3. Paint a sun and a sky, then glue the palace onto one of the hills. Then, cut pink paper roofs and glue them onto the palace.

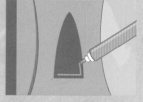

4. Cut windows and doors from paper and glue them onto the palace. Then, draw frames on them with a felt-tip pen.

5. Cut out small paper hearts and glue one onto the top of each roof. Then, paint some trees on the hills in the background.

6. Cut out photographs of flowers from magazines and glue them onto the background. Then, draw stalks and leaves.

Fairy tiara

Only cut halfway into the band.

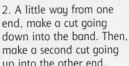

1. Cut a narrow band of thin cardboard that fits once around your head. Then, cut a little off one of the ends.

2. A little way from one end, make a cut going down into the band. Then, make a second cut going up into the other end.

3. Cut six strips of kitchen foil which are twice as wide as the band. Then, squeeze and roll them to make thin sticks.

You could use shiny cardboard for the band.

You can bend the foil sticks in lots of different ways to make different kinds of tiaras.

Try hanging a
paper heart from
a piece of thread.

The tiara sits on the top of
your head. You may need
to clip it to your hair.

4. Cut each stick in half.
Then, bend one piece in
half so that it makes an
arch. Tape it onto the
middle of the band.

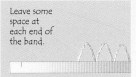

Leave some
space at
each end of
the band.

5. Bend the rest of the foil
sticks into arches. Then,
tape five arches on either
side of the middle one.
Turn the tiara over.

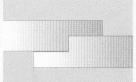

6. Decorate the front of
the tiara with stickers and
sequins. Then, slot its ends
together so that the ends
are inside, like this.

Fairy collage

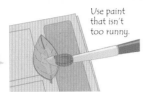

Use paint that isn't too runny.

1. For the wings, lay a small leaf onto some newspaper, with the veins facing up. Then, brush paint over the leaf.

2. Lay the leaf on a piece of tissue paper and press hard all over it with your fingertips. Print six more leaves and let them dry.

You may need to overlap the leaves.

3. Cut out all the printed leaves. Then, cut a pale paper circle for a head. Cut some hair for the fairy from shiny paper.

4. Glue the hair onto the head, and add a face. Then, cut a top and a skirt for the fairy's dress from bright paper.

5. Glue the skirt onto the top. Then, glue three printed leaves onto the skirt. Cut a strip of paper for a sash, and glue it on.

6. From pale paper, cut two arms and glue them onto the back of the body. Then, glue on four leaves for the fairy's wings.

7. Turn the body over and glue it onto a piece of paper, but don't glue the bottom of the skirt yet. Glue on the fairy's head.

8. Cut two shoes from shiny paper and glue them just under the fairy's skirt. Then, glue the bottom of the skirt onto the paper.

You can use any bright or shiny paper, such as wrapping paper, for the dress.

Make fairies with different hairstyles and crowns.

To make a layered skirt, cut an extra layer and glue it underneath.

9. Cut a crown and a wand from shiny paper and glue them onto the fairy. Then, decorate the fairy with lots of shiny stickers.

31

Fairyland caterpillar and flowers

Caterpillar

You don't need the lid.

You could paint spots instead of using stickers.

1. Carefully cut the lid off a cardboard egg carton. Then, cut the bottom part of the carton into two pieces, along its length.

2. To make the caterpillar, paint one piece green, and leave it to dry. Put the other piece to one side, for the flowers.

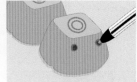

3. Carefully push the point of a ballpoint pen into the front of the caterpillar, like this, to make two holes for its feelers.

4. Push two short pieces of drinking straw through the holes. Then, draw a face. Press stickers all over the caterpillar's body.

Flowers

Make flowers with different petal shapes.

1. For the middles of the flowers, cut the other piece of egg carton into three pieces. Paint them orange and let them dry.

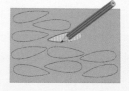

2. Draw a petal on thin cardboard and cut it out. Then, draw around it lots of times on bright paper and cut out the shapes.

3. Turn the orange pieces over and glue the petals onto them, overlapping the petals a little. Then, leave the glue to dry.

4. Scrunch three pieces of yellow tissue paper into balls. Then, glue the balls into the middles of the orange sections.

5. For the stalks, press a piece of poster tack onto the back of each flower. Then, press a straw into the poster tack.

Flower garlands

1. Lay a saucer on some pale pink paper and draw around it. Then, draw around a mug on some bright pink paper.

2. On some white paper, draw around a bottle top. Then, cut out all the circles and glue them together, like this.

To make lots of petals, make more cuts into the circle.

3. For the petals, cut very thin triangles into the biggest circle. Only cut as far as the edge of the bright pink circle.

4. Make more flowers, then cut a drinking straw into short pieces. Tape one piece of straw near the top of each flower.

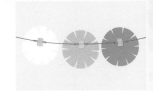

5. With the pieces of straw at the tops of the flowers, thread a long piece of ribbon through them all. Then, hang the flowers up.

Fairy cooking

Spangly heart biscuits

To make about 25 biscuits, you will need:

2 tablespoons caster sugar
pink food colouring
75g (3oz) butter, softened
3 tablespoons light soft brown sugar
3 tablespoons maple syrup
1 medium egg
175g (6oz) plain flour
a medium and a small heart-shaped cutter
two greased baking trays

Heat your oven to 180°C, 350°F, gas mark 4 in step 6.

❀ The biscuits need to be stored in an airtight container and eaten within a week.

Add one spoonful of maple syrup at a time.

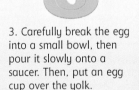

1. Put the caster sugar into a bowl, add two drops of colouring and stir the sugar until it is pink. Then, spread it on a plate to dry.

2. Put the butter and soft brown sugar into a large bowl. Stir them hard until they are creamy, then stir in the maple syrup.

3. Carefully break the egg into a small bowl, then pour it slowly onto a saucer. Then, put an egg cup over the yolk.

Keep the egg white.

4. Hold the egg cup over the yolk and carefully tip the saucer over the small bowl so that the egg white dribbles into it.

5. Add the yolk to the large bowl and mix it in. Sift in the flour and stir it in well, then squeeze the mixture to make a dough.

6. Wrap the dough in plastic foodwrap and put it in the fridge to chill for half an hour. While it is in there, heat your oven.

36

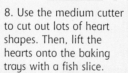

7. Sprinkle a clean work surface with flour. Then, use a rolling pin to roll out the dough until it is about 5mm (¼in) thick.

8. Use the medium cutter to cut out lots of heart shapes. Then, lift the hearts onto the baking trays with a fish slice.

9. Cut holes in the hearts using the small cutter. Then, press the scraps into a ball, roll it out and cut out more hearts.

10. Using a fork, stir the egg white quickly for a few seconds. Brush some onto each biscuit, then sprinkle them with pink sugar.

11. Bake the biscuits for 10-12 minutes, until they start to turn golden brown. Then, carefully lift them out of the oven.

Wear oven gloves.

12. Leave the biscuits on the baking trays for a few minutes. Then, lift them onto a wire rack and leave them to cool.

Pretty fairy fudge

To make about 70 fudge shapes, you will need:

450g (1lb) icing sugar
100g (4oz) pink marshmallows
2 tablespoons milk
100g (4oz) unsalted butter
half a teaspoon of vanilla essence
red food colouring
small cutters
small sweets, for decorating

✿ The fudge needs to be stored in an airtight container in a fridge and eaten within a week.

1. Sift the icing sugar through a sieve into a large bowl. Make a small hollow in the middle of the sugar with a spoon.

2. Using clean scissors, cut the marshmallows in half and put them in a small pan. Add the milk, butter and vanilla essence.

3. Gently heat the pan on a low heat. Stir the mixture every now and then with a wooden spoon until everything has just melted.

4. Pour the mixture into the hollow in the sugar. Mix everything together until it is smooth, then mix in a drop of colouring.

5. Leave the mixture to cool for 10 minutes, then make it into a flattened round shape. Wrap the shape in plastic foodwrap.

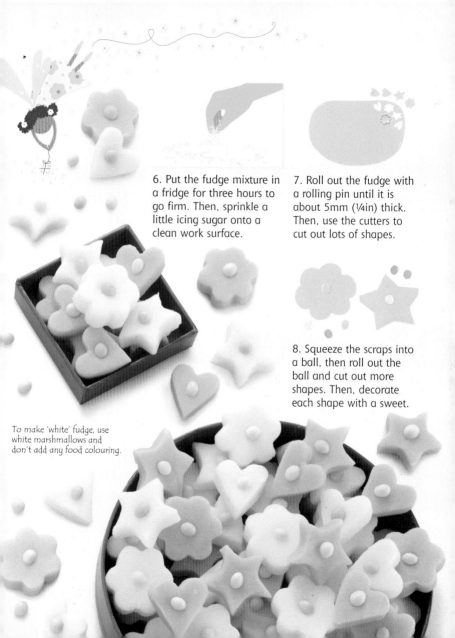

6. Put the fudge mixture in a fridge for three hours to go firm. Then, sprinkle a little icing sugar onto a clean work surface.

7. Roll out the fudge with a rolling pin until it is about 5mm (¼in) thick. Then, use the cutters to cut out lots of shapes.

8. Squeeze the scraps into a ball, then roll out the ball and cut out more shapes. Then, decorate each shape with a sweet.

To make 'white' fudge, use white marshmallows and don't add any food colouring.

Fairy muffins

To make 10 muffins, you will need:

300g (10oz) plain flour
2 teaspoons baking powder
150g (5oz) caster sugar
1 lemon
50g (2oz) butter
225ml (8 fl oz) milk
1 medium egg
100g (4oz) seedless raspberry jam
a 12-hole muffin tin
small sweets and sugar sprinkles, for decorating

For the icing:
175g (6oz) icing sugar
2 tablespoons lemon juice squeezed from
   the lemon from the main mixture

Heat your oven to 200°C, 400°F, gas mark 6
before you start.

❀ The muffins need to be stored in an airtight container and
should be eaten on the day you make them.

Use a pastry
brush.

If you are having
a birthday party,
you could decorate
some of the muffins
with little candles.

1. Brush some oil in ten of
the muffin holes. Then, cut
a small circle of baking
parchment to put in the
bottom of each hole.

2. Sift the flour and baking
powder into a large bowl.
Add the caster sugar, then
mix everything together
with a metal spoon.

Use a lemon squeezer.

Heat the pan gently.

3. Grate the rind from the lemon using the medium holes on a grater. Then, cut the lemon in half and squeeze the juice from it.

4. Put two tablespoons of juice on one side, for the icing. Then, cut the butter into pieces and put it in a pan with the lemon rind.

5. Add four tablespoons of milk and heat the pan until the butter melts. Then, take it off the heat and add the rest of the milk.

6. Break the egg into a cup and mix it well with a fork, then stir it into the butter mixture. Then, add the mixture to the bowl.

7. Stir everything together with a fork. Then, nearly fill each muffin hole with the mixture and bake the muffins for 15 minutes.

8. Leave the muffins in the tin for three minutes, then loosen them with a blunt knife. Then, put them onto a wire rack to cool.

Use a sharp knife.

9. Turn each muffin on its side and cut it in half. Then, spread jam on the bottom half and lay the top half on top.

10. Sift the icing sugar into a bowl and mix in the lemon juice. Then, spoon icing onto the muffins and press on some sweets.

Swirly pink biscuits

To make about 40 biscuits, you will need:

75g (3oz) icing sugar
150g (5oz) butter, softened
1 lemon
200g (7oz) plain flour
2 tablespoons milk
pink food colouring
two greased baking trays

Heat your oven to 180°C, 350°F, gas mark 4.

✿ The biscuits need to be stored in
an airtight container and eaten
within a week.

1. Using a sieve, sift the
icing sugar into a large
bowl. Add the butter and
mix it in until the mixture
is smooth and creamy.

2. Grate the rind from a
lemon using the fine holes
on a grater. Then, add the
rind to the creamy mixture
and stir it in.

42

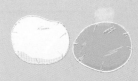

3. Put half of the mixture in another bowl. Sift half of the flour into each bowl, then add a tablespoon of milk to each one.

4. Add three drops of colouring to one of the bowls. Then, squeeze each mixture to make two balls of dough.

5. Flatten the balls of dough a little and wrap them in plastic foodwrap. Put them in the fridge for 30 minutes to chill.

6. Sprinkle flour on a clean work surface, then roll out the plain dough until it is about 25 x 15cm (10 x 6in) and 5mm (¼in) thick.

7. Roll out the pink dough until it is about the same size as the plain dough. Then, brush the plain dough with a little water.

8. Carefully lift the pink dough and lay it on the plain dough. Then, use a sharp knife to make the edges straight.

The layers of dough make a spiral when you roll them.

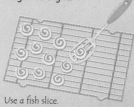

Use a fish slice.

9. Roll up the dough from one of the long sides. Then, wrap it in plastic foodwrap and chill it in the fridge for 30 minutes.

10. Turn on your oven. Then, cut the rolled-up dough into 5mm (¼in) slices and put the slices on the baking trays.

11. Bake the biscuits for 12-15 minutes. Leave them on the baking trays for two minutes, then lift them onto a wire rack to cool.

Mini fairy pastries

To make 24 pastries, you will need:

375g (13oz) packet of ready-rolled puff pastry
1 medium red onion
1 tablespoon of olive oil
half a teaspoon of dried mixed herbs
a pinch of salt and of ground black pepper
12 small cherry tomatoes, washed
150g (5oz) mozzarella cheese
1 tablespoon of milk
2 baking trays

Heat your oven to 220°C, 425°F, gas mark 7 before you start.

❀ Leave the pastries to cool for five minutes, before you eat them.

1. Take the pastry out of the fridge and leave it out for 15-20 minutes. Then, carefully cut the ends off the onion.

2. Peel the onion and cut it in half. Then, cut each half into two pieces. Very carefully cut each piece into thin slices.

3. Gently heat the olive oil in a frying pan. Then, add the onion and stir it every now and then for about five minutes.

4. Remove the pan from the heat and stir in the herbs, salt and pepper. Then, unroll the pastry and cut it into 24 squares.

5. Put the squares on the baking trays, leaving spaces between them. Prick the middle of each square twice with a fork.

6. Open the mozzarella bag and pour away any liquid. Cut the mozzarella into tiny cubes. Then, cut the tomatoes in half.

7. Pour the milk into a mug. Then, brush milk around the edge of each square, making a border about 1cm (½in) wide.

8. Spoon some of the onion and herb mixture onto each square, making sure you don't cover the milk border.

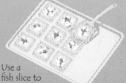

Use a fish slice to remove them.

9. Put half a tomato onto the top of each square. Then, scatter a few cubes of mozzarella on top of each one.

10. Cook the pastries for 12-15 minutes. When the edges have risen and turned golden, the pastries are cooked.

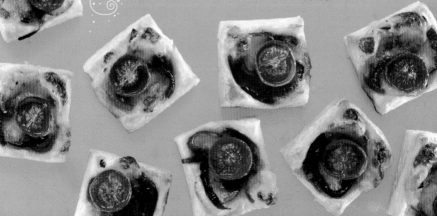

Pretty fairy star biscuits

To make about 25 biscuits, you will need:

350g (12oz) plain flour
2 teaspoons ground ginger
1 teaspoon of bicarbonate of soda
100g (4oz) butter
175g (6oz) soft light brown sugar
1 medium egg

4 tablespoons golden syrup
writing icing
small sweets, for decorating
a large star-shaped cutter
2 greased baking trays

Heat your oven to 190°C, 375°F, gas mark 5
before you start.

❀ The biscuits need to be stored in a single layer in
an airtight container and eaten within five days.

1. Sift the flour through a
sieve into a large bowl.
Then, sift the ginger and
bicarbonate of soda into
the bowl, too.

2. Cut the butter into
chunks with a blunt knife.
Then, add it to the bowl
and stir it in so that it is
coated with the flour.

3. Rub the butter into
the flour with your fingers,
until the mixture is like fine
breadcrumbs. Then, stir in
the sugar.

4. Break the egg into a
small bowl, then add the
syrup. Beat them together
well with a fork, then stir
the mixture into the flour.

5. Mix everything together
until you make a dough.
Then, sprinkle a clean work
surface with flour and put
the dough onto it.

6. Using your hands, push
the dough away from you
and fold it over. Do this
again and again until the
dough is smooth.

7. Sprinkle more flour onto the work surface, then roll out the dough until it is 5mm (¼in) thick. Use the cutter to cut out stars.

The cookies will be golden.

Stick on single sweets with a dot of icing.

8. Lift the stars onto the baking trays. Squeeze the scraps into a ball, then roll the ball out and cut out more stars.

9. Bake the biscuits for 12-15 minutes. Carefully lift them out of the oven and leave them on the baking trays for five minutes.

10. Put the biscuits onto a wire rack to cool. When they are cold, decorate them with writing icing and press on small sweets.

Flowery cut-out biscuits

To make about 10 biscuits, you will need:

100g (4oz) butter, softened
50g (2oz) caster sugar
a small orange
1 medium egg
2 tablespoons ground almonds*
200g (7oz) plain flour

1 tablespoon of cornflour
8 tablespoons seedless
   raspberry jam
a 5cm (2in) round cutter
a small flower cutter
2 greased baking trays

Heat your oven to 180°C, 350°F, gas mark 4 in step 6.

❀ The biscuits need to be eaten on the day you make them.

* Don't give these biscuits to anyone who is allergic to nuts.

1. Put the butter and sugar into a large bowl. Mix them together with a wooden spoon until the mixture looks creamy.

2. Grate the rind from the orange using the medium holes on a grater. Then, add the rind to the bowl and stir it in.

3. Break the egg into a cup and mix it with a fork. Then, add a little of the egg to the creamy mixture and mix it in well.

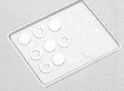

4. Add some more egg to the bowl and mix it in. Carry on until you have added all the egg, then add the ground almonds.

5. Sift the flour and cornflour into the bowl. Then, mix everything with your hands until you have made a dough.

6. Wrap the dough in plastic foodwrap and put it in a fridge to chill for 30 minutes. While it is in there, heat your oven.

7. Sprinkle some flour onto a clean work surface. Then, use a rolling pin to roll out the dough until it is about 3mm (⅛in) thick.

8. Using the round cutter, cut out lots of circles. Then, use the flower cutter to cut holes in the middle of half of the circles.

9. Squeeze the scraps into a ball. Then, roll out the ball and cut out more circles. Put all the circles onto the baking trays.

The biscuits turn golden brown.

10. Bake the biscuits for 15 minutes. Leave them on the baking trays for two minutes, then move them onto a wire rack to cool.

11. Spread jam over the whole biscuits, as far as the edge. Then, place a flower biscuit on each one and press it down gently.

Tiny fairy cakes

To make about 24 fairy cakes, you will need:

1 medium egg
50g (2oz) self-raising flour
40g (1½oz) soft margarine
40g (1½oz) caster sugar
small paper cases
a baking tray

Heat your oven to 180°C, 350°F,
gas mark 4 before you start.

✿ The cakes need to be stored in
  an airtight container and eaten
  within four days.

For the icing:
50g (2oz) icing sugar
about 1 tablespoon of warm water
pink food colouring
small sweets and sugar sprinkles, for decorating

Use a wooden spoon.

1. Break the egg into a mug.
Then, sift the flour into a
large bowl, through a sieve.
Add the egg, caster sugar
and magarine to the bowl.

2. Stir everything together
well, until the mixture is
smooth and creamy. Then,
put 24 paper cases onto
the baking tray.

The cakes will
turn golden brown.

3. Spoon some of the cake
mixture into the paper
cases, using a teaspoon.
Each case should be just
under half full.

4. Bake the cakes for about
12 minutes, then carefully
take them out of the oven.
Lift the cakes onto a wire
rack to cool.

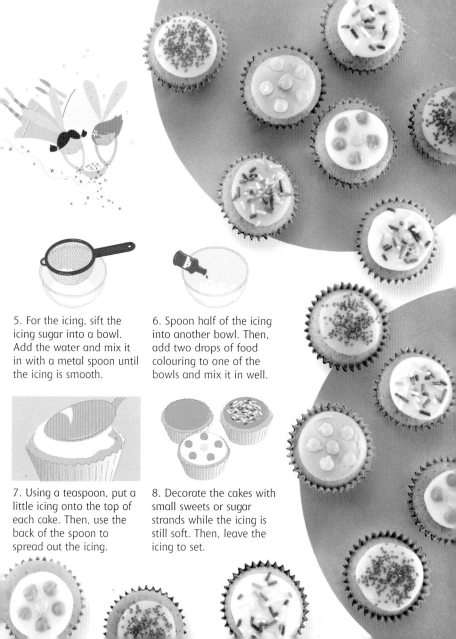

5. For the icing, sift the icing sugar into a bowl. Add the water and mix it in with a metal spoon until the icing is smooth.

6. Spoon half of the icing into another bowl. Then, add two drops of food colouring to one of the bowls and mix it in well.

7. Using a teaspoon, put a little icing onto the top of each cake. Then, use the back of the spoon to spread out the icing.

8. Decorate the cakes with small sweets or sugar strands while the icing is still soft. Then, leave the icing to set.

Iced raspberry mousse

To make 4 mousses, you will need:

150g (5oz) raspberries
4 tablespoons icing sugar, sifted
4 tablespoons Greek-style yogurt
150ml (¼ pint) double cream
25g (1oz) meringues*
fresh raspberries and small mint leaves,
   to decorate
four 150ml (¼ pint) ramekin dishes

✿ The mousses need to be stored in a freezer and
eaten as soon as you have decorated them.

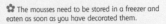

1. Put the raspberries into
a bowl and mash them
with a fork until they are
squashed. Then, add the
icing sugar to the bowl.

2. Stir the raspberries and
icing sugar to mix them.
Then, add the yogurt and
stir it in until everything is
mixed together.

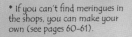

* If you can't find meringues in
the shops, you can make your
own (see pages 60–61).

52

3. Pour the cream into a bowl. Then, use a whisk to whisk the cream until it is thick and there are points when you lift the whisk.

4. Add the yogurt mixture to the cream. Then, gently turn the mixture over and over with a spoon, to mix everything together.

5. Carry on until the whole mixture is pink. Then, break the meringues into small pieces. Add them to the mixture and stir them in.

6. Spoon the mixture into the dishes. Then, put the dishes into a freezer for two hours, or until the mousses have frozen solid.

7. Take the frozen mousses out of the freezer. Then, decorate each mousse with a fresh raspberry and two mint leaves.

53

Cut-out sandwiches

To make 3 sandwiches, you will need:

6 slices of bread
thin slices of ham
butter or margarine
a cucumber
strawberry, raspberry or apricot jam
a large round cutter and a small cutter

✿ Eat the sandwiches as soon as you've made them,
or wrap them in plastic foodwrap and store them in
a fridge for up to six hours.

Ham sandwich

1. Lay a slice of bread on a chopping board. Place the round cutter on it and press hard. Then, remove the cut-out circle.

2. Cut another circle from a second slice of bread. Then, use the small cutter to cut a shape in one of the circles.

3. Lay the round cutter on top of a slice of ham. Then, very carefully cut around the cutter with a sharp knife.

4. Spread butter on one side of each bread circle. Then, lay the ham on the whole circle and lay the circle with the hole on top.

54

If you're having a party, make lots of sandwiches
in different shapes and with different fillings.

Cucumber sandwich

1. Cut two bread circles
and cut a hole in one
of them. Then, slice the
cucumber until you have
lots of thin slices.

2. Spread butter on the
bread circles and lay slices
of cucumber on the whole
one. Then, lay the circle
with the hole on top.

Jam

Cut two bread circles and
cut a hole in one of them.
Spread butter and jam on
the whole one, then press
the circles together.

Butterfly cakes

To make 8 cakes, you will need:

1 medium egg
50g (2oz) self-raising flour
quarter of a teaspoon of baking powder
50g (2oz) caster sugar
50g (2oz) soft margarine
paper cake cases
a baking tray with shallow pans

For the butter icing:
40g (1½oz) butter, softened
a few drops vanilla essence
75g (3oz) icing sugar, sifted
about 4 teaspoons seedless
   raspberry jam
extra icing sugar, for dusting

Heat your oven to 190°C, 375°F,
gas mark 5 before you start.

✿ The cakes need to be eaten on
the day you make them.

1. Break the egg into a mug.
Use a sieve to sift the flour
and baking powder into a
large bowl. Add the egg,
caster sugar and margarine.

2. Stir all the ingredients
together with a wooden
spoon. Carry on until you
have made a smooth
creamy mixture.

3. Put eight paper cases
into the pans in the baking
tray. Then, use a teaspoon
to half fill each case with
the mixture.

56

Wear oven gloves.

Use a wooden spoon.

4. Bake the cakes for 16-18 minutes. Then, carefully lift them out of the oven and put them onto a wire rack to cool.

5. To make the icing, put the butter into a bowl and add the vanilla. Stir them together until the mixture is really creamy.

6. Add some of the icing sugar to the butter and stir it in. Add the remaining icing sugar a little at a time, stirring it in each time.

Leave an edge around the circle.

7. Using a sharp knife, carefully cut a circle from the top of each cake. Then, cut each circle in half, across the middle.

8. Spread some of the icing on top of each cake. Then, carefully spoon half a teaspoon of jam in a line across the icing.

9. Gently push two of the half slices into the icing, so that they look like butterfly wings. Then, sift a little icing sugar over the top.

Little cheese scones

To make about 16 scones, you will need:

40g (1½oz) Cheddar cheese
175g (6oz) self-raising flour
half a level teaspoon of baking powder
a pinch of salt
25g (1oz) butter
100ml (4 fl oz) milk
milk, for glazing
4cm (1½in) round and heart-shaped cutters
a greased baking tray

Eat the scones
as they are or cut
them in half and spread
them with a little
butter.

Heat your oven to 220°C, 425°F, gas mark 7, before you start.

✿ Eat the scones warm or store them in an airtight container
and eat them within three days.

1. Grate the cheese using
the medium holes on a
grater. Then, sift the flour,
baking powder and salt
into a large bowl.

2. Cut the butter into small
pieces and add them to
the bowl. Then, rub them
in until the mixture looks
like fine breadcrumbs.

3. Mix in the grated cheese
with your hands and pour
in the milk. Then, use a
blunt knife to mix
everything together well.

4. Gently press the mixture
together with your hands
to make a soft dough.
Then, sprinkle flour onto
a clean work surface.

5. Using a rolling pin, roll out the dough until it is about 1cm (½in) thick. Then, use the cutters to cut out circles and hearts.

6. Squeeze the leftover scraps of dough into a ball and roll it out. Cut out more shapes, until you have used all of the dough.

7. Put the shapes on the baking tray, leaving spaces between them. Then, brush the tops of them with a little milk.

Some of these scones had a little plain flour or grated cheese sprinkled onto them, before they were baked.

8. Bake the scones for seven to eight minutes, until they rise and turn golden. Then, lift them onto a wire rack to cool.

Mini meringues

To make about 15 white and 15 pink mini meringues, you will need:

2 eggs, at room temperature
100g (4oz) caster sugar
pink food colouring
150ml (¼ pint) double cream
2 baking trays, lined with baking parchment

Heat your oven to 110°C, 225°F, gas mark ¼ before you start.

✿ The meringues need to be stored in an airtight container and eaten within a week. Once you have filled them, eat them on the same day.

You could use a yolk to make confetti cookies (see pages 62-63).

1. Carefully break one egg on the edge of a small bowl, then pour it slowly onto a saucer. Put an egg cup over the yolk.

2. Hold the egg cup over the yolk and carefully tip the saucer over the bowl so that the egg white dribbles into it.

3. Repeat these steps with the other egg, so that the two egg whites are in the bowl. You don't need the yolks in this recipe.

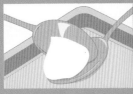

4. Whisk the egg whites with a whisk until they are really thick. They should form stiff points when you lift the whisk up.

5. Add a heaped teaspoon of sugar to the egg whites and whisk it in well. Repeat this until you have added all the sugar.

6. Scoop up a teaspoon of the meringue mixture. Then, use another teaspoon to push it off onto the baking tray.

Use a metal spoon.

7. Make 15 meringues, leaving gaps between them. Then, add four drops of food colouring to the rest of the mixture.

8. Gently mix in the food colouring by turning the mixture over slowly. Then, when the mixture is pink, make 15 more meringues.

9. Put the meringues in the oven and bake them for 40 minutes. Then, turn off the oven, leaving the meringues inside.

Wear oven gloves.

10. After 15 minutes, carefully lift the baking trays out of the oven. Leave the meringues on the trays to cool.

11. Pour the cream into a small bowl, then strongly whisk it with a whisk. Carry on until the cream is quite thick.

12. Using a blunt knife, spread some cream on the flat side of a meringue. Then, press another meringue on the top.

Confetti cookies

To make about 100 cookies, you will need:

50g (2oz) butter, softened
75g (3oz) caster sugar
1 egg yolk
1 teaspoon of clear honey
1 teaspoon of vanilla essence
2 teaspoons milk
100g (4oz) plain flour
25g (1oz) cornflour
2 greased baking trays
small cutters

You could use lots of different shaped cutters for the cookies.

For the icing:
150g (5oz) icing sugar
2 tablespoons warm water
pink food colouring

Heat your oven to 180°C, 350°F, gas mark 4 before you start.

✿ The cookies need to be stored in a single layer in an airtight container and eaten within three days.

Use a wooden spoon.

1. Put the butter and sugar into a large bowl. Beat them until they look creamy, then add the egg yolk and beat it in.

2. Stir in the honey, vanilla essence and milk. Sift the flour and cornflour into the bowl, then start to mix everything with a spoon.

3. Use your hands to squeeze the mixture until you make a ball of dough. If the mixture is a little dry, add a drop of milk.

4. Sprinkle a work surface with flour, then roll out the dough until it is about 5mm (¼in) thick. Use the cutters to cut out shapes.

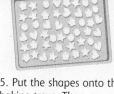

5. Put the shapes onto the baking trays. Then, squeeze the scraps into a ball, roll the ball out and cut out more shapes.

The cookies turn golden brown.

6. Bake the shapes for six to eight minutes, then carefully lift them out of the oven. Leave them to cool on the baking trays.

7. To make icing, sift the icing sugar into a bowl and mix in the water. Then, spoon half of the icing into another bowl.

8. Cover one bowl with plastic foodwrap to stop it drying out. Then, mix two drops of food colouring into the other bowl.

Use a blunt knife.

9. Spread half of the cookies with white icing. Then, spread the others with pink icing and leave the icing to set.

Marzipan toadstools

To make 8 toadstools, you will need:

250g (9oz) 'white' marzipan*
red food colouring

❁ The toadstools need to be stored in an airtight container and eaten within three weeks.

1. Cut the block of marzipan in half. Then, wrap one half in plastic foodwrap and put the other half in a small bowl.

2. Add three drops of colouring to the bowl and mix it in with your fingers. Then, break the marzipan into eight pieces.

3. Roll each piece into a ball, then squash them to make toadstool shapes. Press your thumb into the bottom to make a hollow.

Wash your hands first.

4. Unwrap the other half of the marzipan. To make spots, break off a third of the marzipan and roll it into lots of little balls.

5. Press several of the little balls onto each toadstool. Then, break the remaining piece of marzipan into eight pieces.

6. Roll each piece between your fingers to make a stalk. Then, press a red top onto each stalk to complete the toadstool.

Editor: Leonie Pratt   Series editor: Fiona Watt   Art director: Mary Cartwright
Photographic manipulation: Emma Julings.   Images of flowers on pages 26-27 © Digital Vision.
First published in 2005 by Usborne Publishing Ltd., Usborne House, 83-85 Saffron Hill, London, England. www.usborne.com Copyright © 2005, 2003 Usborne Publishing Ltd.
The name Usborne and the devices ♀ ♥ are Trade Marks of Usborne Publishing Ltd. All rights reserved. No part of this publication may be reproduced, stored in a retrieval system, or transmitted in any form or by any means, electronic, mechanical, photocopying, recording or otherwise without the prior permission of the publisher. Printed in Dubai.